It was Rudyard Kipling who wrote, "Make ye no truce with Adam-zad, the Bear that walks like a Man!"* His message was clear, but there is a haunting drama buried within it—the spirit of the wild animal, intriguing, unapproachable, forever remote from mankind. By its very nature the phenomenon of wildness possesses a deep fascination for many people. One tries to contemplate what it is, why it is, how impenetrable it is.

Did you ever have a secret longing to live with a lion, or elephant, or bear or any other wild animal, in order to know what they are really like? Extension of a childhood fantasy? Perhaps. But fantasies remain only fantasies until they are realized, then they become adventures.

When Molly came to us she was a five and a half pound clump of fur and claws. One year later we had a beautiful Malayan sun bear, fully grown at 125 pounds. At no

i

time was she ever in a cage or on a leash. We roamed the woods together like two characters out of a Kipling tale. She climbed the trees, ran with the dogs, delighted the children, fascinated the plumber, got into mischief, and lived an existence that was unique. But what stood out about Molly, above all, was her incredibly honest, innocent manner.

Bears do not understand complex things like fences, stairs, windows, lamps, clotheslines, furniture, vehicles... they do comprehend the significance of decaying apples under a tree, a stream of fresh water, flat rocks covering a cluster of ants, scratches on a tree which tell of another bear's presence. Their nose and ears are the conduit to their surroundings. So then must the wild, primitive, self-contained mind form a non-relating existence to the humans who control the planet on which it roams.

This book is intended to be more than an intimate diary of a pet bear's adventures. It is also an attempt to reveal the cold, harsh reality of unfairly kidnapping a wild creature away from the world in which it belongs, for the sake of human needs, ego-related or otherwise. Those few individuals who do harbor the fanatical dedication necessary to

MOLLY AND ME

The Story of a Bear

Daniel Samuels

To my wife, Iris,
and our children
who shared this special experience
as an integral part of our family life

and to

all those who harbor
a reverence for animals.

MOLLY AND ME
The Story of a Bear

Published by Daniel Samuels Copyright ©
1997/2020 by Daniel Samuels

Book design: Harry LeMay
Cover illustration: Nancy LeMay

CONTENTS

PREFACE

succeed must inevitably be the first to realize the fallacy of the elusive dream.

The author hopes the reader will enjoy the story of how we raised a wild animal, appreciate it, sympathize with it and, above all, not contemplate a similar venture.

"The Truce of the Bear"

CHAPTER I

AIRPORT RENDEZVOUS

A bleak drizzly April morning. But it didn't matter. In fact the rest of the world was forgotten on that long-waited day as I neared Kennedy Airport. I was en route to pick up my bear.

Why me? Why a bear? It starts with a visit to the zoo in early childhood, where something gets planted. Then you read some books, see some movies, go back to the zoo, read more books, repeat the cycle.

You grow up, but the captivation is still there; in fact, more firmly entrenched. You continue to visit the zoo; by now you've made friends with the keepers, which enables you to spend a glorious summer there working with the animals.

Then you get married to a girl who was already mildly fond of animals but now has been proselytized into liking them even more. She works with you that memorable summer at the zoo. You take your honeymoon in East Africa and stay there a few weeks, foreseeing (rightly) that it will be the only time when you are young and free to pursue such vagabond adventures.

AIRPORT RENDEZVOUS

Seeing the animals living free in the wild has a profound effect on you. You wish you could get closer to them, touch them, but you realize you can't. You like them and quixotically want them to like you back, but you know animals well enough by now to realize this is fantasizing, You recall the time you ran after a young giraffe on the plains of Tsavo but couldn't get close to him. Or the time you walked amongst the 5000 lb. white rhinos in a back country village call Rumeruti—you remember referring to them as "merely big rabbits."

So you drift around, take some pictures, and appreciate this ephemeral, intermission before returning home to find a job and take your place on the treadmill of suburban living.

Seven years later. Now we have three children and a house in the country with enough acreage for... an animal of some kind. What will it be? We don't have a suitable location nor space for a lion or other big cat; besides neighbors could never accept that type of resident in their vicinity. A hoofed animal such as a zebra or giraffe would have to have heated quarters during the winter, and would require a long, initial quarantine period. Chimps, after they mature, tend to become unhappy in a captive, mateless existence (can you blame them?). The animal should be one that would not be too out of place on a few acres of land and woods.

It eventually narrowed down to three possibilities—spotted hyena, African hunting dog (sometimes called a cape hunting dog) or a small species of bear.

I was well acquainted with the first two from my African involvement and always had a particularly sympathetic feeling for them, since both have been so wrongfully maligned through the years because of their natural habits in the wild. Tradition based on ignorance creates such attitudes.

The hunting dog and the hyena are both highly gregarious animals, living in large clans (matriarchal) where a well-defined social order exists. Both have been raised with domestic dogs where the physical similarities offer grounds for substantial compatibility.

The animal dealers were no problem to find in those days for one familiar with the zoological trade. Today it is more difficult for one to acquire an exotic animal (as it should be).

A hyena was not available. I had asked for a female hyena pup though actually it is almost impossible to distinguish a male from a female in a very young hyena; both resemble males (!)—an interesting curiosity.

There was a female hunting dog available which I was about to accept when, at the last minute, the telegram from Singapore arrived. The sun bear can be sent to someone genuinely interested in "raising it." I chose the bear. The price—not much more than for a 19" television.

My reaction was one of sharply mixed emotions. First, there was the great anticipation of the childhood dream of living close to a wild animal, studying it, trying to befriend it. In contrast to this was the cold, sober intellectual awareness that no one should own a bear or any wild animal—they aren't meant to be owned.

With this constantly in mind, I was all the more determined to mitigate this sacrilege against nature by making sure that my bear would be spared, in every possible way, the usual miseries of confinement. No bars would ever imprison her, no chain or leash relegate her to a lackluster, sedentary non-existence.

The name was already chosen—Molly. I don't know where it came from, except that it seemed a cute name for a bear. In later months, we would think of an even better name—Stuffy, suggested by the bulging chest of the slightly over-fed ten-month-old bear, but it would be too late by then. Molly it was, and Molly she remained.

The longed for rendezvous was about to take place. All the years of wishing and waiting had converged into a single, electric moment at an airport freight terminal.

Then I saw here. The little black form was just partially visible through the mesh of a small box cage. She wasn't much bigger than the pint-sized water can secured in one corner of the enclosure.

I unwrapped the wires, opened the cage lid and gently lifted her out. There she was in my arms—five and a half pounds of *ursus Helarctos malayanus*, the Malayan Sun Bear. I estimated her age at six to seven weeks. The fur was short and smooth; the curved claws seemed long for such a little animal. On her chest was the characteristic yellow "V" which is the identification tag of all sun bears. I confirmed that all-important marking much as the mother of a newborn baby makers an instant count of ten fingers and ten toes. After all there are several other types of bears in Southeastern Asia, and the others are all considerably larger than the sun bear when full-grown. By the time the sun bear reaches adulthood the chest marking will be halfway between a "V" and a "U."

The tiny cub's eyes showed no facility of recognition. It wouldn't be meaningful to say she was or wasn't frightened, for at such a young age a bear cub is little more than a detached embryo. The body odor had a distinct sweetness unlike any familiar scent. But it was not disagreeable at all; wouldn't have been even to an impartial observer, which I certainly was not.

It is said that the name sun bear is derived from the chest design supposedly resembling either a setting or rising sun (take your choice), but the alleged similarity has never been apparent to me.

Actually, all bears are very small when born; even the largest types produce tiny cubs. How intriguing to contemplate that a nine hundred pound polar bear or fourteen hundred pound brown bear weighed only one and a half pounds at birth. The ratio of adult weight to birth weight in bears must rank as the highest of any large mammals. The newborn of other animals in the thousand pound class, such as the horse or cow, weigh at least thirty pounds. Some marsupials, such as the opossum, are even smaller than bears at birth, weighing as little as two ounces, but they are equipped with a ready-made incubator, namely the pouch, with which to sustain the diminutive new-comer.

The human infant at six to seven pounds starts off almost 400% larger than the bear cub, but the rates of growth and development between the two represent complete extremes of nature. At the end of one year the cub will have grown to a self-sufficient one hundred pounds plus, while the still totally dependent human baby will only be around twenty pounds.

It should be noted that there are several animals which are referred to as "bears" but are actually not in the bear family. The honey bear, more formally known as the *kinkajou cercoleptinae*, belongs instead to the Procyonine family (along with the racoon and the greater panda, among others). Many people are surprised to learn that the well-known "Koala bear," *phascolartidae* from Australia, is really not a bear, but a marsupial —possessing a pouch like a kangaroo. As in the case of the honey bear, the Koala is furry and roly-poly so that a cursory appraisal might indicate resemblance to a bear cub, but a brief side-by-side comparison would readily show that it has very little similarity to a real bear. The nose, ears and paws are easily seen to be quite different.

For Molly the long-term process of relating to people was to begin immediately. She would make the fifty-mile ride to our house tucked inside my windbreaker jacket. The weather was cold and raw so the arrangement was most appropriate. With little more than her nose sticking out, the cub seemed to welcome the reassuring bundling.

We were off. Down the parkways of Queens, over the Whitestone Bridge, up through the east Bronx, and on into Westchester County. The towns slowly rolled by. Mount Vernon, New Rochelle, Mamaroneck, Rye. As we gradually made the transition from crowded suburbia to open country I felt a little more at ease. Back in the milling turmoil of the metropolitan area, the thought of a flat tire or some traffic accident had loomed as the most ominous example of the wrong thing at the wrong time. At last we were home!

Molly became the instant center of attraction in the house. The girls, Adrienne and Bonnie, who were to become bear experts at ages seven and five, respectively, were delighted to have another animal to love and care for. My wife, Iris, welcomed Molly with the rest of us, though expressing some concerns as to whether the relatively large claws would pose a problem with Howard, the baby, who was only a year old.

The dogs, Bogo and Betsy, ran alongside me eagerly jumping up to investigate the strange new animal. As I placed her on the bedroom rug, they sniffed excitedly not knowing what to make of their new companion, who was unlike anything they had ever come across before.

I wanted so much for the adoption to be successful, aware of course, that is was a considerable strain on nature's laws to ask a bear to live with people. Predictably there would be problems in the beginning; the one that plagued us the most was the bad case of diarrhea that stubbornly persisted from the start. I knew it was not unusual for this condition to arise from the sudden change in diet, but I was also aware that it could produce a serious problem of dehydration if it lasted too long. Feeding was by bottle, and was not without temper tantrums often seen in young wild animals.

Betsy became an instant stepmother, proceeding to lick Molly all about the head and body as if the cub were her own puppy. On another occasion Betsy did the same thing to a tiny kitten who eventually grew up to be an everlasting companion. As was to be later seen Molly also became very devoted to Betsy although her method of showing it
(bites and mauling) was not so obvious to those uninitiated in the ways of bears, including Betsy.

CHAPTER II

THE WAY OF THE WILD

The largest selling automobile in the United States in the late sixties was the (Chevrolet) Impala, named after an African antelope whose picturesque bounding leaps are a unique phenomenon of the animal world.

This is an example of how often in our lives we encounter some identification with animals. They are found not only in children's stories but in much of our adult culture as well. Automobiles are named after them, as well as athletic teams, political mascots, and even the stock market trend. We see them in ads and TV commercials, usually extolling some desirable physical attributes such as power, speed or grace. Their furs are worn (unfortunately) as a symbol of beauty. There are cosmetic styles to give "that feline look," "that gazelle-like look," etc.

Animals are loved by some people, feared by others, regarded casually by most. Domestic animals share a coexistence with man which centers about their servitude to him. They provide food or other by-products, labor or companionship that can, on occasion, become an intense, lasting attachment.

But what is there about the wild animal that distinguishes it from others? What fuels the instinct to remain aloof from humans?Dictionary definitions are given as thus:

Wild: Living in a state of nature; not ordinarily tame or domesticated.

Tame: To reduce from a wild to a domestic state; to make gentle or tractable; to bring under control.

This definition may be somewhat confusing since it contains the world "domestic," but the meaning for its derivative, "domesticate," suggests a deeper intimacy with man—

Domesticate: To adapt an animal or plant to life in intimate association with, and to the advantage of man; to live in the same household, to settle in, or become habituated to an ordered household.

Some zoologists regard wildness as a genetic property, a built-in quality, which can fade away only after thousands (or even millions) of years of exposure to man, The dog, cat, horse, cow, pig, sheep, and goat are all sufficiently domesticated to live in harmony with man, yet every one of them originally derived from wild ancestors, and, in fact, still has relatives today in the feral state. Certainly it is the dog, however, which has established the closet bond with humans and is the only animal that consciously seeks the approval of man. Just when or how the dog made the evolutionary transition from wild to tame has not been determined—it may go back to the Neanderthal man.

One can raise a young animal such as a deer or squirrel so that it will allow itself to be hand-fed. The animal is then said to be "tame," that is, the basic fear of people has been overcome to the extent that it can be approached, but that is still a long way from being truly domesticated.

The layman might reasonably wonder if a totally wild animal like a bear could be made tame by indulging in a program of extreme kindness right from the beginning. Would it accomplish anything, for example, if the cub were literally hugged, kissed and thoroughly coddled every day?

It turns out that such techniques are insufficient to overcome completely that "built-in" wildness which makes itself evident in the animal's ability (or inability) to relate to humans.

Bears particularly among wild animals seem to live in a world of their own which is impervious to rational logic. It can be seen in their eyes, where the expression shows little recognition of human overtures. Furthermore, they do not welcome handling or petting, although this is true of most young, wild animals. Those animals which we think of as "cuddly," often represented by children's toys, such as the Koala bear, panda, honey bear, lion cub, etc. are as it turns out not this way in real life. Being held frightens them and while they may tolerate it for a short time, the end result is often a scratch or a bite. It usually takes several months before the animals begin to lose that instinctive fear, and even then handling in never really welcomed as it is with a dog.

In the case of young bears one has to contend with temper tantrums during the first six months of age, and Molly was no exception. These consist of screaming, biting rages which end as suddenly as they began. Anything that frustrates the bear can bring on the tantrum. It is first noticed at the bottle-feeding stage where, if the drink is not made available quickly enough, the eruption occurs. The occasional incidents we hear about between bears and visitors to national parks illustrate this point.

In general, withholding or running out of food (bears do not distinguish between the two) is a personal relations disaster to anyone attempting to establish a rapport with a bear. If the public were more aware of this, there would be fewer of those incidents which sometimes happen when people attempt to feed bears.

As long as the supply holds out a park bear is content to accept food, and there is little danger if no attempt is made to handle the animal. However, when the morsels are gone the bears simply do not understand why no more is forthcoming, and they become resentful. They seem to assume that the donor still has more and is deliberately withholding it. That is when trouble can begin.

Some tourists, besides unwisely lingering after the food is gone, may further compound the error by attempting to pet the bear. After all, they reason, he is now grateful for the meal and will certainly not object to an obvious token of friendship —but unfortunately this is more of a case of wishful thinking than reality.

With a wild animal there is really no such thing as "grateful." That response is simply not part of their emotional repertory (though the ancient story of Androcles might suggest otherwise). Furthermore, the act of petting, to a wild animal, constitutes an aggressive gesture, likely to incur defensive reactions of varied magnitudes.

The bear is then said to be "unpredictable." Actually, anyone familiar with the way of bears could have predicted a seemingly unexpected anger tantrum. Too often zoologists will label an animal "unpredictable" because it didn't react to a given situation as a human being would have.

Therefore, since the success of bear feeding is dependent upon good technique, it is definitely not to be recommended, and, understandably, park authorities discourage the practice though their warnings are not always heeded.

Among wild animals there are various degrees of tameness that can be achieved. Some, particularly big cats, tend to become one-man animals, that is, they are most tolerant of the person who has fed them, cared for them, in other words brought them up. It is also important to realize that within a given species there are wide variations of behavior. Fred Martini, who cared for the large cats at the New York Zoological Park for more than a quarter century and who, along with his wife, Helen, raised lions, tigers, and leopards in their home, told me of the large variations he observed among individuals within a given species. Each animal had its own distinct personality. Whereas one may be gentle and sociable, the next may be a completely different temperament.

The idea is often advanced that a harbored wild animal may "suddenly revert" and cause a disaster. This is an over-simplification which sounds exciting, but isn't necessarily a foregone conclusion. I personally do not subscribe to the "time bomb" theory. Again, it depends on the type of animal, the individual animal itself, and the overall attitude and dedication of the person.

How ridiculous it is to make lions, bears, or what have you, jump through hoops, ride bicycles, roll a ball, walk a tightrope, etc., as in circuses. It isn't that difficult to turn an animal into a robot by offering a reward. I have seen rhinoceroses brought up by humans that were so tame that one could walk up and pet them (p.102).

Even the reputedly fearsome adult rhino tames fairly easily if one has the patience, technique and dedication required to do the job. This little-known fact was described by the late A.T. Richie, former Chief Game Warden of Kenya for 25 years, who had a special interest in rhinos and was considered an outstanding authority on them. The noted author on African wildlife, Jean Pierre Hallet, tamed an adult rhino fairly easily while living in the Belgian Congo (now Zaire). He also had a pet lion, cape buffalo, and hyena among others. Hyenas, incidentally, have been found to make intelligent, trustworthy pets if gotten young enough. This endeavor has been described in detail by a Nairobi man named Croydon who wrote an article on the subject in the wildlife magazine *Africana* in 1966.

I cite these examples merely to show it can be done. This is definitely *not* to suggest that it is desirable to impose on wild animals the precondition that they fraternize with humans. Such an objective is unfair to the animal because it robs it of its natural, intended existence. Those of us with a deep feeling for nature cannot escape some feelings of guilt about doing this.

We can try to rationalize by imagining that the animal might not have lived as long or eaten as well, or had such security, but it still gnaws at our conscience—the idea that the animal has been taken out of the wild and subjected to an artificial life.

So, where Molly was concerned, at least she would be brought up in a setting close to her natural one. She would have space to roam in, trees to climb, insects to eat, and loads of companionship (animal and human) and the greater catalyst of all, kindness—to which we were sure she would respond. Time would tell.

Bonnie, Adrienne & Molly. Respective ages: four, six, two months.

WITH THE GRANDMOTHERS
The girls and my mother.

Iris' mother with Adrienne and one-year-old Howard.

CHAPTER III

KITCHEN CONNOISSEUR

After one week our little cub had established a set routine of eat, play and sleep. Her formula consisted of evaporated milk, egg yolk, and rice pablum which she took well; however the diarrhea still persisted. I had tried Kaopectate, which didn't help, and was quite upset over my failure to get rid of the condition. Finally I called a prominent zoo veterinarian who happened to live in my county. It was a Sunday morning, apparently the wrong time to bother such an individual about a bear's diarrhea. After firing a vituperative tirade at me, Dr. G. hung up in my face—and I still had learned nothing. Nevertheless I was confident that gradually her system would adjust to the diet, and continued to keep careful notes on it. Eventually the problem did disappear.

Ten days after she had come we brought Molly outside for the first time. She liked the new experience immediately began exploring everything—deep grass, rocks, woods. The instinct to follow was quite evident, for she would trail whichever dog was closer to her.

The desire to climb was also there right from the beginning; rocks, bushes, chairs, anything, just had to be climbed. She seemed practically drawn to tree trunks, which is not surprising since trees are such an important part of a sun bear's life. Her first attempt at tree climbing consisted of going up about three feet and then lingering. I felt inclined to assist her down and tried to gently lift her off the trunk. This was met with loud defensive growls followed by a bite just as she was being released on the ground, confirming that young wild animals simply despise being picked up. There was no doubt, however, that it was more difficult for Moll to descend a tree than climb it. Left to her own resources she would work her way down with great difficulty.

With each new climbing attempt Molly gained more confidence, but then came the day when it got her into trouble. She had gone up a front-lawn tree that measured about ten feet to the first branch, and then must have started thinking about the long trip downward. She was stuck, just like a kitten that has to be rescued. She didn't like the situation one bit and let it be known by issuing a series of roars that were worthy of a hundred pound lion. It was hard to believe such amplitude could come from that tiny an animal.

I hurried to the garage for the stepladder in order to effect a rescue. In the meantime the loud bellowing continued and when I did climb up to her, predictably she resisted my efforts to assist. But that is how it is with a wild animal—help them and get assaulted for it. Needless to say, my arms took plenty of punishment on the way down, but you don't fault a wild animal for being what it is. Ten months later Molly, then ninety pounds, was to meet me again at the top of the stepladder for cookies—each of us climbing from opposite directions. The photo shows who went via the steps (the easy way) and who was relegated to the rung (p. 106).

The days went on; each one saw the little cub adapting more and more to her life with us. The diarrhea had disappeared and everything was fine. Before long Molly had acquired several nicknames. "Molly-Pie" or sometimes just "Pie" for short, or "Moll." She played for long periods with Betsy who perfectly fit the role of foster mother. The "game" consisted mostly of Molly plunging into Betsy with hardy bites. Although she had her thick winter coat, Betsy still did not always appreciate the mauling, and made retaliatory snaps when it was too persistent.

Adrienne and Bonnie's teddy bear moved by itself. Bears have prominent claws right from birth.

We knew it was desirable for the cub to have a furry mother substitute, particularly a dog who had already had her own litter of pups. Bogo, the male dog, showed scant interest in the bear, and avoided her most of the time as he would his own offspring.

At about ten weeks of age Molly lapped milk from a plate for the first time. She still used the nipple when she was hungry, and continued to roar if milk didn't come fast enough. Gradually, though she began to make the transition from bottle to plate, after which I started giving her baby cereals and dog food. The latter was to become her main diet supplemented by fruits, cookies and insects.

After her feeding we would bring Molly outside where, as if on schedule, she would promptly "go to the bathroom." It was interesting to note that she always urinated and defecated simultaneously, a habit I had also observed in African elephants.

Inside the house Molly was quite active, always climbing and/or biting something. Like teething puppies, she would bite just about anything—furniture, shoes, toys, etc. Unlike the domestic dog, however, the mature bear does not lose the instinct to bite objects—and what the teeth can't mangle the claws probably will. A cushion chair, for example, left in a room or field with a bear would be completely shredded in half an hour.

It was amusing to watch Molly and year-old Howard, each crawling toward the other on what looked like a sure collision course, but at the last minute one of them (usually Molly) would veer off, and each would continue on his own way. We always called that particular scene "ships in the night."

Molly was quite small (seven pounds five ounces) when she first negotiated the six steps between our ground and second floors. Since it is always easier to an animal to climb up than go down, it was a full two weeks later before Molly, then at eleven and a half pounds, was able to go all the way down the stairs.

After feeding she was inevitably very occupied either playing with Betsy or investigating any convenient attraction, but always in the room where the people were. She took over the kitchen, not only for the food, but also for the appliances which intrigued her. If the dishwasher was left open she would climb in, frivolously enjoying the rides on the sliding parts. In later months she would stand up on two legs and spring the opening latch by herself, making use of that well developed dexterity that bears seem to possess.

Another source of rides was the refrigerator door. Her technique there was to pry the door open (it was the magnetic type with no latch) and then cling tightly as its inertia would provide a long swing to the adjacent wall. After this maneuver was executed, the food was next on the agenda. Molly quickly learned that long curved claws are ideal for extracting roller-type shelves harboring all kinds of delicious tidbits. One of her favorite items was the oleomargarine container. The lid was pried off and the contents happily devoured, that is, if I did not intervene, which I had to do in most cases to preserve our food supply. On those other occasions when I left her alone it was understood that the food was being sacrificed in the name of "behavioral research." Molly's favorite dog food was kept in the cupboard, and it didn't take her long to find that out. She came across it on the first shelf-climbing excursion, and from then on always remembered that important fact.

The procedure there was to climb three shelves, send the carton falling to the floor after which she would tear the outer cardboard, then the individual box and finally the cellophane bag to get the food. Such a sequence of operations again shows the complex manipulations a bear is capable of.

One of the most unforgettable sights occurred when Iris, working in the kitchen, looked around to find Milly sitting in the double-size bread drawer busily appropriating all the cookies within reach. The incredible thing was how she ever got up there, for being just three months old the bear was only fifteen inches long, and weighed a mere thirteen pounds. The drawer was at least twenty inches off the ground so that it had been necessary for her to pull out the lower drawer first, and haul herself into it. Of course drawer pulling comes quite easily to bears with their natural equipment well suited for it.

It was interesting to note that while Molly would invariably eat food which had been acquired by climbing to an out-of-the-way place, she would often ignore the same food if it were offered in her feeding plate. This trait is sometimes seen in other animals, such as the house cat, which is often more likely to show interest in food which has been "stolen" than the same food made freely available.

Another favorite kitchen pastime of Molly's was to maul the towels and sponges found in the other drawers. The maulings consisted of biting, clawing and vigorously shaking the object in question, which often ended up being contributed in the name of "science" like the oleomargarine previously noted.

KITCHEN CONNOISSEUR

CHAPTER IV

WHAT'S A POTTO?

There was no doubt that Molly caused a big change in our lives; she was the constant center of attention. Companionship, close and continuous, was to be the all-important catalyst in getting her to relate to us.

Many people imagine that is a carefree novelty to own a wild animal, but in reality the exact opposite is true. Those who acquire a lion cub, for example, may have a delightful time for a couple of months showing it off and gaining the sought-after notoriety. But before long the novelty wears off and the rapidly growing animal begins to represent a tiresome chore, then an outright burden. Young animals often tend to be quite destructive around a house, and their presence usually becomes too great a strain to be withstood indefinitely.

How many times in the past could one see an ad in the Sunday "New York Times" which typically read "Lion cub, 5. mo. old, tame, wonderful with children, must sell." The last two words in the ad were the tip-off —of course they had to sell because they had no idea whatsoever what they were getting themselves into.

While he has an exotic pet there are any number of devices the exotic pet exhibitionist can use to draw attention to himself. For example he can nonchalantly walk down the street with the lion on a leash knowing he will shortly be on center stage. Or he can resort to a more subtle ploy such as leaving the animal in a car within a crowded parking lot where it will be sure to be noticed. Surreptitiously watching the proceedings from a suitable distance, he will return amongst the commotion while feigning beleaguered innocence. He secretly hopes that someone has called the police. Maybe the press and television media, eager for something novel, will send reporters to the scene and, with a little luck, the seeker of instant fame may end up having his picture shown across the country—the ideal antidote to the prospect of being a perpetual nonentity. The danger of losing the pet by having it confiscated may even be worth the notoriety achieved.

I knew a man affiliated with a nearby Humane Society which had "acquired"—that is, rescued—a young bear from a "pet" store. In a well-meaning if not naive endeavor, he brought the six month old, thirty pound cub home, his intention being to keep the bear with his family for a while until a "suitable" home could be found. The pipe dream lasted exactly three days, after which the cub was unceremoniously returned to the society's quarters. Like many others who tried similar ventures he hadn't realized what he was in for. Seventy-two hours of biting, scratching, house wrecking, and various other forms of non-relating was all the family could endure.

The story had an unfortunate ending for the bear reportedly ended up in a small zoo in northeastern Pennsylvania, when it could have been reunited with its own kind in the Malaysian jungle. At our initial meeting the director of the society agreed to let me try to make arrangements to have the bear returned to the wild, as was similarly done with the lion, Elsa, in the "Born Free" story. The society had hoped to benefit from the resultant publicity which would have been considerable in those days when the ecology movement was at its peak.

I even got to appear with the bear on the Dick Cavett Show and implore the public not to acquire wild animals for pets. Dick Cavett impressed me as having a genuine concern for animals. During the twenty minute interview I barely managed to keep the cub preoccupied with bread, cookies, and a jar of honey. The honey had spilled creating quite a mess, and frequently the television monitors showed close-ups of the bear's snout smeared and dripping in olio, a sight thoroughly enjoyed by the audience.

When it was time for me to leave, I stood up and started to carry my frisky bundle off the stage. He didn't like being removed from the food and went into a tantrum, biting me hard on the left hand. For someone supposedly familiar with bears I really messed that up. The scar is still visible.

As an interesting sidelight, the night before we were on that show, Senator and former presidential candidate Hubert Humphrey had been the guest. It was amusing to eventually learn that our segment of the program had achieved a higher Hooper rating than Humphry's did!

After several months of considerable effort I achieved just what we were hoping for—the bear could be rehabilitated to a southeastern Asian jungle, and a television producer was willing to film the project! The game warden of Sabah (formerly British North Borneo), Mr. G. S. de Silva, agreed to accept the bear for such a purpose. (I still have his letter.) There could have been no better person to be in charge of the project for Mr. de Silva was a superb, dedicated preservationist who had already won acclaim for his outstanding work in saving orangutans and sea turtles. He had also successfully returned sun bears to the wild in the Sepilok Forest Reserve of Sabah—of course the sun bear is indigenous to that area.

Wolfgang Bayer, the executive producer for Bill Burred Productions, indicated that he would like to film the rehabilitation project for his "Animal World" series (in my opinion the best of the many wildlife series on television throughout the seventies), so it looked as if we were all set. The plan was to make a prominent example of this return to the wild, while at the same time emphasizing how wrong it is to take the animals out of their native habitat in the first place. The project seemed too good to be true; then the bubble burst.

Unfortunately greed and mercenary priorities began to emerge as the Humane Society director suddenly insisted on $2000 before turning over the bear, claiming "boarding charges" which, in truth, were insignificant. What really happened was that a small Pennsylvania zoo had offered over

$1000 for the bear, the money to be raised by a public campaign. Thus all my work was for naught, but the really disheartening aspect of the story was that a "Humane Society" (located in New Jersey) should end up sacrificing its scruples for an immediate payoff. The national publicity they would have received could have been used to augment contributions for the worthy cause.

It has always been too easy for unqualified people to acquire wild animals. This is the fault of the pet industry which steadfastly opposes any corrective legislation that would prevent these abuses. Perhaps one out of 50,000 people is equipped physically and emotionally to harbor a wild animal. An intense dedication is absolutely essential. Even for me at times it was a strain because of the enormous responsibility which was there every day of the year.

Since we never had any restraint, such as a leash, on Molly we had to keep an eye on her outside. When she played in the woods I would check on her whereabouts every few minutes. Usually I could either see her through the foliage or hear her rustling about in the brush. Those times when I could not locate her I would go into the woods to check further.

WHAT'S A POTTO?

One day I had a very unpleasant scare when I failed to find her as usual. I raced feverishly around her regular haunts but she was nowhere to be seen. All the fears we had ever entertained came to mind as I visualized newspaper headlines proclaiming, "Bear Found in Armonk"... etc. It was just by sheer luck that I happened to glance up and spot her high in a tree. For some reason it had not occurred to me that she might have climbed but, needless to say, from that time on I always made a thorough check of the trees whenever searching for my roaming bear.

The sun bear is a natural tree climber all its life, as opposed to the larger bears that climb only the first year or eighteen months after which they rarely do because they become too heavy. Molly liked to sit at the junction of major branches which formed a tripod-like seat, and claw and bite at the bark. She would usually descend after a half hour, but I recall the first occasion when she stayed up well over an hour. It was getting dark and dinner was on the table but I couldn't get her down. I tried all the usual tricks, such as pretending to leave, but to no avail. There was nothing else to do but stand under the tree, flashlight in hand, and wait.

Finally she came down, and unceremoniously followed me into the house. In the future months I realized that it was not necessary to wait for her as I had done. Left alone in the woods she invariably returned to the house via the back door.

One memorable afternoon she came lumbering into the kitchen covered with yellow jackets which she had acquired in the woods. There must have been a dozen of them imbedded in various places. The ones on her back and chest did not appear to sting her for her fur, thin as it was compared to that of other bears, was still heavy enough to afford protection. The ones on her snout, however, were able to sting and they required immediate attention. Her technique was to bat them off with her paw and matter-of-factly eat them. I gingerly removed the others with no appreciation from her—in fact she acted as if I were molesting her—and gave them to her to be promptly gobbled up.

Bears love to eat insects; it is a natural food for them. What a sight it was to see Molly turn over a rock and lick up hordes of crawling ants. The girls used to obtain black ants by leaving a lollipop outside. They would then collect them in an oleomargarine cup after which they would bring it to Moll who would lap up the ants in a matter of seconds with a vacuum hose type operation. Like many insect eaters the sun bear has a surprisingly long tongue. Sometimes during a yawn it could be seen to extend over twelve inches.

As far as neighbors were concerned there was no trouble; we were fortunate in that respect for in our situation it would have taken just one with an opposing philosophy to make life miserable for us. Of course Molly was rarely very far from our property which certainly didn't hurt out cause.

There was one family in the vicinity that I had some doubts about so when they subsequently inquired, "What the heck is that?" I replied that she was a "potto." Certainly few people outside of the zoological field have ever heard of a potto, a rather obscure animal found in West Africa.

I correctly anticipated that they would head straight for the library where they would find that a potto is a small, furry, tree climbing animal, roly-poly in appearance— not unlike a bear cub, at least to a layman. One thing I hadn't counted on was that they would stumble onto the fact that pottos have spiny protrusions in the back of the neck which form defense mechanism when used in a butting motion. They informed me of their research and questioned how much of a danger she would pose because of the spinal minihorn! I assured them that such a threat was quite minimal, and no further problems arose although they did remain skeptical for a while. At least it was better than telling them that they lived pretty close to a real bear.

CHAPTER V

MOLLY'S ROOM

At four months of age Molly was given her own sleeping quarters. It was an extra room in the basement, which was ideal, since it had some high shelves where Molly always preferred to sleep. I also put in some wooden boards to aid her climbing to the shelves.

Of course nothing valuable could be left in the room because Molly could completely destroy anything she could reach, and given the climbing ability of a sun bear there was virtually nothing she couldn't reach.

In the mornings when I would come into her room to feed her, then take her outside, Moll would invariably greet me with profuse licking on my face and neck, accompanied by a constant chirping sound. This non-stop caressing often lasted as long as three minutes; she would first cover one side of my face and neck and then the other side. Only after that ritual was finished would she begin to feed.

The chirping was one of three sounds that Molly could make. The others were a roar and a bark, both of which were rarely heard. The roar was forthcoming if something greatly frustrated her, such as that first time she got stuck in the tree. The bark was emitted only if she were abruptly frightened —if, for example, a big dog had run around the house and confronted her unexpectedly. Of course it was the dog who invariably got the bigger surprise. Molly's bark was loud and deep—virtually indistinguishable from that of a large dog. I don't recall hearing it more than three times in the space of a year.

While Molly had no fear of dogs—in fact she liked them and always wanted to meet them—their barking seemed to frighten her, and would cause her to head instantly for the nearest tree. I sometimes made use of that trait when trying to get her to climb for visitors, by engaging Betsy in a tug-of-war with a towel. Like most terriers, Betsy would growl vigorously as she pulled against me, and Molly would just keep climbing until she was about forty feet up. If I were at the base of the tree when she descended, Molly would invariably pull one of her favorite tricks. She would maneuver to a point just above me then release her forearms and plummet down on me forcing me to carry her.

MOLLY'S ROOM

She would do the same thing whenever I stood under the "cave" shelf in her room, dropping down on me with her full weight. This habit was the cause of an accident which was the only time she ever really hurt me, completely unintentionally, of course.

There was an old bureau in her room which Molly used to climb after pulling the drawers out; I would often find her curled up on top of it. Our routine was well established. I would go over to her and she would climb on my shoulders to be lowered to the floor.

On one occasion when Moll was eight months old and weighed about sixty-five pounds, she suddenly hopped onto my shoulders before I was ready, causing me to lose my balance and stagger back. This in turn made Molly tumble off me and as she started to fall she instinctively clung to the nearest object, which unfortunately happened to be my face.

The resulting claw marks went from my cheekbone all around the rear of my neck like three ski trails, deep and painful. I pushed her aside and stumbled upstairs for medication. It was two months before the scars finally disappeared. It is important to realize that, as already noted, this injury was entirely unintentional. A house cat would have done exactly the same thing it if were falling; the difference is that a sixty-five pound animal does a lot more damage than one of ten pounds.

Afterwards, with the benefit of hindsight I realized that I should have immediately fallen down with Molly, and in that way would have avoided the mishap. She never did hurt me again though we played mauling games every day of the year. One reason was that I got to know her movements so well—how the front paws swiped, how the back paws raked or clung, how the "bowling ball" head moved, where the spaces were between her teeth—but the all-important aspect is that she had absolutely no inclination to purposely hurt after the six month tantrum period had passed.

The one precaution I had to take in playing with Molly was to guard my eyes, and this was done by firmly clasping my hands over them. Simply closing them was not good enough to protect against gouging from claws, head, nose canine teeth, etc. I have found the same practice necessary when playing with a lively dog.

Our technique of play became so perfected that on hot summer days I would maul with Moll without any shirt on! I must confess that I wouldn't have gone out of my way to do it if it hadn't been for the extreme heat. Her claws did make me wince at times but I accommodated by learning how to roll with the scratching movements. In the cooler weather I sometimes used another ploy in the same situation, going into a tight chest-to-chest clinch as a boxer does to slow down his opponent's momentum.

It was interesting to note that Molly would often attempt to maul me by circling around to sneak up from behind. If I pretended to be unaware of the goings on, she would plunge into my back and bite vigorously about the shoulder blades. Even as a small cub the instinct to stalk from the rear was present. That was only one of literally dozens of behavior patterns I learned to recognize. As the months went by my whole family gradually was becoming experts on the habits of the Malayan sun bear.

CHAPTER VI

DIARY OF A SPRING DAY

Morning. Still, asleep on the high shelf.

Half awake, hear noise of someone moving in the house. Climb down to the lower shelf in anticipation of the morning visit and feeding time.

On guard—someone coming down the steps—you know who it probably is. The door opens, in walks Dan with cellophane bags of dog food and apples. He puts the food on the floor.

The face to face greeting takes place. Lots of chirping and licking, then a tumble onto chest and shoulders to be routinely lowered to the floor. Ignore the food for a few moments and continue the greeting.

The "necking" subsides; turn the attention to the filled plate. Good food. Typical bear stance while eating, front paws in an exaggerated pigeon-toed alignment—back ones almost straight, maybe a tiny bit inward also. The rapt gaze showing complete engrossment in feeding.

Food all gone. Time to get moving. Out the door, through the garage, stop for a long drink of cool, fresh water from the tub which cannot be left in your room because it would be tipped over.

Moving fast now, a running gait, out the rear garage door, bounding across the backyard. Stop to go to the "bathroom." Both functions at the same time. For the duration of the bowel movement the front left paw is held straight outward.

Lots of things to do in the woods—feel very much at home there. Sniff like a dog at the base of a tree, paw around the earth, lick up any ants or beetles which are dislodged. Move on to another tree for more of the same.

Rather abruptly walk right up the tree as if it were on level ground. Take the first pause at fifteen feet to sniff at something interesting, then continue up to a height of almost thirty feet and sit on a natural tripod. Almost out of sight as you diligently nibble leaf buds and claw at the bark on the main trunk. The single-minded purpose of your endeavor makes you totally oblivious to the pair of blue jays which linger for a few moments to shriek protests at the unexpected invader of their domain.

Twenty minutes later move on, up to a higher point closer to the top of the tree. Now more visible from the ground than before since you emerged from the dense foliage where you were sitting. The rays of the rising sun form a brilliant gold aura on your chest mark.

Finally head down the tree. The decent is much quicker than the climb, less than two minutes, with only brief contemplative stops along the way. Back on the ground again. Forage around, then spot Dan watching nearby trying to be unobtrusive. Show that you're not ready to come in by scurrying further into the woods.

After forty minutes of unmolested privacy, start back by retracing pretty much the outgoing route. Very little lingering on the way back as the intent to return is definite. At the edge of the woods now. There's Betsy looking at nothing in particular. She doesn't notice her friend. Suddenly stop and stalk her from behind. Doesn't work for long—Betsy easily hears the noise and turns placidly, her stubby tail beginning a slow wag. Since you've been discovered there's nothing better to do than turn the stalk into a full-scale charge. Go barreling headlong at Betsy and upon reaching her flail vigorously with both paws while rocking the head from side to side.

None of the blows land solidly as Betsy, wise you your mischievous ways, scrambles out of range with a perfunctory growl. Any presumption of indignation is dispelled by the still wagging tail. Across the field Bogo watches with an expression that suggests, "What's that nut up to now?"

No one else to rough up so back to the house, through the garage. Another drinking session at the water tub, then into the room for some bread and cookies already waiting. After the eats, climb up to the "cave" shelf for a two-hour nap.

Out again in the late afternoon. Everything pretty much a repeat of the morning odyssey. Once again back to the security of the room for the evening feeding. At eight o'clock in come the playmates— Adrienne, Bonnie and Danny. You alternately maul, nip and chirp as everyone strokes your fur and tugs at your jowls, The girls love the antics of their real life teddy bear, continually proclaiming how smart and precious you are.

Finally time for them to leave. Everyone kisses you goodnight while you climb up for the last cookie snack. Another day passed with these people who are trying to make your life with them as idyllic as possible.

Two young ladies in the garden.

The consequences of being spotted at an open window.

With Adrienne.

Pretzel time.

Sharing cookies with Howard.

CHAPTER VII

BEAR HUG

Someone once said, "When you hug a bear, who hugs who?" (grammar not withstanding). Curiously enough, there is no such thing as a "bear hug." Bears do not hug, they cling, so that the only "bear hugs" to be found are in a wrestling match.

It is also interesting to note that a bear is not a clawing animal in an aggressive sense. Certainly you will be thoroughly scratched in any encounter with one, but the scratching is a by-product of swatting and clutching done by the paws. A bear is strictly a biter, and uses his claws to pull the adversary within range of the jaws; he does not intentionally use his claws for the purpose of scratching, as does any cat.

There was one particular instance when I actually was the recipient of the mythical bear hug. We had been wandering in the woods near the house late on a summer afternoon, and I decided to sit on a large rock just inside the edge of the woods while Molly foraged nearby in her usual manner. Eventually her movements brought her alongside me, whereupon I anticipated the customary nip followed by a hasty retreat; instead, Molly stood up, clamped her head against my back for several moments. It was a fairy-tale scene, a zoological anomaly—but it did happen.

I reached around and scruffed her hooded neck; satisfied, she dropped down and moved on. Could this have been a special attempt at communication on man's terms instead of a bears? I don't really know, but I was elated to find out that Iris had seen this unique incident from the kitchen window. At least there was one witness to a story that doesn't sound very likely but will live forever in my memory.

If one were to ask any number of experienced zoologists or animal "handlers" what the prospects were of successfully raising and maintaining a sun bear, the unanimous (and reasonable) answer would be—impossible! Everyone usually has at least one disaster story to tell as proof that such things can't be done. Certainly I agree that, normally, it should never be tried—for the animal's sake.

I recall an incident told me by Bill Conway, Director of the New York Zoological Society (Bronx Zoo), about a sun bear that seriously clawed his keeper of ten or more years, but the details of that story made it clear to me that the mishap was a "clinging" accident, similar to the pone I had had. Admittedly it may not have been that much consolation for the keeper to know that the act was not done out of malice.

Actually, it is meaningless to compare the performance of a caged zoo animal with that of our Molly, who lived a much freer and more natural existence. Moreover, Molly had intensive amounts of human companionship, not a token few minutes such as a zoo animal might receive, usually through the bars of a cage. The observations of zoo-oriented "experts" must therefore be read with a certain degree of caution, even those of a man as renowned in the field as the late Dr. Lee S. Crandall, Director of the Bronx Zoo for many years and a diligent compiler of data. For example, writing on young sun bears in "Management of Wild Animals in Captivity," the "bible" of zoos (at least through the seventies), Crandall states, "Unfortunately, however, their playfulness (i.e., of the young cubs—D.S.) soon gives way to the irascible temper of the adult, which certainly is among the most ill-natured of bears." In our case where a dedicated effort was made to allow the bear to relate to humans, we found the exact opposite to be true. The older Molly got the milder she became. At a year and a half, she showed practically none of the aggression of her adolescence. A striking example of this was in the way my 75-year-old mother could always fondle Moll at will with no adverse reaction on the part of the latter—the only casualty being some silk stockings which were not particularly claw-resistant.

Even Iris' mother, a lady in her fifties, strictly from the big city—she'd never been on a farm—had an excellent rapport with the bear. She would always visit Molly first thing upon entering the house and spoil her with cookies and other goodies calculated to make an already fat bear more overweight.

In a similar vein, the same zoological reference cited above also describes the alleged ferocity in captivity of the anoa, a small water buffalo trying to maintain survival on its native Indonesian island of Celebes. Zoo keepers, it is reported, are said to give them "a wide berth at all times." I once befriended an anoa in a zoo, later went into his pen on countless occasions and found him completely friendly—virtually incapable of aggression. I couldn't get him to charge me even if I tried (p. 99).

The children, of course, were completely at home with Molly, but after she started getting bigger (above seventy pounds) I preferred not to leave her alone with them, because the roughhouse, mauling play she was accustomed to was too vigorous for the small children. On some occasions I had to interfere to prevent her from mauling Howard, who was only two years old and certainly couldn't cope with her pugnacity.

It was interesting to compare Molly's behavior with that of a seventy-pound polar bear cub shown in a 1978 television documentary called "White Bear." The bear was being raised by a Russian zoo family which included a girl of about seven.

Betsy—Molly's stepmother.

I marveled (enviously) at the way the cub and child frolicked together, rolling as one down a hill. Later they napped side by side with the cub's snout resting below the girl's cheek. It almost made me feel as if these people had better technique than I, but that wasn't the case for it just wasn't within Molly's scope to relate to such a degree. Nor would she do other things performed by bears on television like "Gentle Ben" (black bear) or "Grizzly Adams" (grizzly). I realized this when I discovered that I could not maintain her in any room of the house without the room being wrecked.

Seven months old and thriving in the summer.

In my opinion, discounting the influence of size, the sun bear is actually wilder than any other species of bear with the possible exception of the sloth bear from India and Sri Lanka (however many are left). What I have read and hear suggest that the sloth bear's extra long claws (necessary for insect excavation) and non-relating temperament combine to give it a minimum compatibility with humans. Such a quality should not be a case for indictment, but should instead be understood and respected. That's the way it was in our house with Molly.

The girls, Adrienne and Bonnie, knew very well how to handle Moll, but the kind of play she liked made it difficult especially with her active claws. What a delightful scene it made when the children played on their swings and seesaw while Moll roamed in the tree which arched high above them. She would stay up for as much as forty minutes at a stretch provided none of us left the area. But if anyone headed for the house (especially I) she would promptly come down. Obviously, she didn't care to be left alone in that situation.

There were a few trees on our grounds upon which Molly inflicted considerable damage from her climbing, mauling sprees. Two evergreens in front of the house and a cherry tree and peach tree in the back were the hardest hit, with some of their main branches broken.

In the case of the fruit trees it did not appear to be the fruit itself which lured Moll to the tree. She rarely showed much interest in eating the peaches or cherries which is more than I could say for the birds. There were times when she nibbled some apples from the apple trees, but just those which had fallen to the ground. The only other wild fruit she ate was some small blackberry clusters which grew on the fringe of the woods. Accordingly, the berries have her droppings a bluish tint.

Apparently, Molly's scant interest in wild fruit was due to the fact that she was always well fed, and therefore did not have to depend on it as a wild bear would. Insects, however, were a different story; she would eagerly lap up clusters of ants or beetles until none remained. She would never eat worms, slugs or flies, but relished bees, yellow jackets, wasps, moths, and some spiders. Obviously not all insects were palatable to her however; once in a while she would hastily spit out a beetle or spider after sampling it.

She also had a great appetite for termites, and was invariably attracted to rotting remnants of trees in the woods where the prospects of such a meal were excellent. Since the termites were mostly inside the wood, Molly bit and clawed her way to get at them. The white gypsy moths which inundated our section of the country in the late 1960's was a very tasty bonus whenever she would find them caught in the grass. Like the blueberries, they also had a pronounced effect on her droppings, in this case bleaching them to a much lighter shade than usual.

Woods, foliage, insects, warm weather—they were all "the name of the game" as far as the sun bear is concerned. The summer was indeed a happy time for all of us.

Sharing a drink with Betsy.

BEAR HUG

"Who's been sitting in MY chair?"

CHAPTER 8

THE DENTIST CALLS

Molly was always enthralled by dogs. Actually, it was a mutual fascination, for the dogs didn't know what to make of the bear. Certainly, they had never encountered anything like her before. Molly would approach them cautiously on all four legs then sometimes rise to the standing position when the dog was about six feet away. In those instances where the dog stayed long enough for them to meet face-to-face, the two would tentatively sniff each other after which Molly would start to paw at the dog's snout. Such a greeting predictably created a negative impression, particularly in view of Molly's foreboding claws, and the canine would quickly move on.

I always had the feeling that whenever Molly stood on her hind legs in that confronting manner, she seemed to think that she as was tall as the sky; her head would be raised with the little chest thrust out and paws lurching in a stance reminiscent of the Frankenstein monster. If the object of this display failed to by intimidated, Molly appeared at a loss to understand how that could be. However most of the time it achieved its purpose with the neighborhood dogs who were thoroughly cowed and would usually flee, after which our little girl seemed to reflect that this was as it should be.

On one occasion when she was about four months old, a family visited us and brought along their young Doberman Pinscher. Moll fixed her gaze on him as he approached then suddenly gave out her rarely heard loud bark, frightening the poor dog out of his wits. Needless to say, he vacated the premises in a hurry.

Our neighbor's dog, Frisky, a beautiful, gentle collie, tended to avoid getting involved with Molly as did most of the dogs who knew her. The fact that she was not afraid of dogs like most animals they would encounter (cat, squirrel, birds, etc.) undoubtedly made a big difference. An animal which runs in fear from a dog almost invariably gets chased.

Like a dog, Molly always enjoyed a nice steak bone. In the beginning, Betsy or Bogo would easily steal it from her by luring her away for play, and then darting around to snatch it. After a while, however, Moll was smart enough to carry the bone up a tree where she could eat it unmolested.

Unfortunately, she tended to be clumsy in handling it and usually dropped it to the ground where the dogs were waiting to immediately confiscate it.

It was interesting to note the different attitudes toward food between bear and dog. Most dogs will display obvious signs of displeasure if one tries to interfere while they are eating a juicy bone; the twitching, retracted upper lip and low growl are sufficient warning of their anger. Molly, however, never showed the slightest sign of resentment in the same situation. Instead she would follow the bone if it were picked up, and do no more than matter-of-factly crowd the interloper out of the way.

The reverse, however, is the case in their reactions when someone feeding them runs out of food. The dog will sit patiently and wait for more, but as noted earlier, the bear will become highly indignant and usually be inclined to search the donor for more.

If there is any weakness in a bear's makeup, it is in the teeth which do not seem sturdy enough to withstand the demands put on them. Bears love to bite things, which causes the teeth to wear down as well as subjecting the enamel to cracking. In addition, bears have an affinity for sweet foods such as honey and berries which must have a deleterious effect on the teeth. Consequently, bears are undoubtedly prone to toothaches which may affect their disposition in the wild. If they only had the teeth of a hyena, they would be better equipped to serve their needs. Nature gave the hyena very strong teeth to go with the most powerful jaws in the animal world.

Like the hyena, bears are a combination of scavengers and predator. While the hyena is mainly (but not exclusively) a carnivore, the bear is totally omnivorous, including in its diet just about anything that is convenient, depending on what is available at any particular time of the year.

As we came to find out, Molly was not without her dental problems. It was at nine months of age when she lost her lower right canine tooth. I noticed it suddenly missing during one of our roughhouse sessions and thought I might have knocked it out, though I couldn't understand how. The break was not a clean one, for some tooth chip was still visible in the gum. I felt terrible and didn't know what to do. The gum was bloody and, of course, Molly resisted any efforts to aid her.

THE DENTIST CALLS

I tried to find a veterinarian who could help, but it wasn't easy to locate one who was willing to examine a bear. Finally, I found someone twenty miles away who had once extracted a lion's tooth in a zoo and was willing to make the trip, for a substantial price of course.

The dentist's visit turned into a three-way wrestling match, with me trying to hold Molly's mouth open while the doctor gingerly tried to get a grip with his forceps. To my great relief, the remaining fragments of tooth came out as soon as the doctor touched it. I managed to find the main part of the tooth on the floor. It was obvious from the decay at its base that it was intended to come out; in short, out Moll was teething!Actually, the new tooth could already be seen, just breaking through the gum. I was overjoyed to learn that I was not responsible for her losing the tooth.

The four canine teeth were the only "baby" teeth, surprisingly, that were replaced by permanent ones. Undoubtedly in the wild where there is no one to help, the remaining tooth chips are pushed out by the incoming tooth. My removing the residue portions did cause the irritation to clear up sooner.

An interesting sidelight to this story is that a prominent zoological "authority," whom I had occasion to meet, was completely unaware (in fact, virtually refused to believe) that the sun bear loses, then replaces, only the four canine teeth. But in fairness to these eminent (and indubitably well-intentioned) experts, it should be remembered that their experience is often limited to what they can do and observe with an animal perpetually behind bars. Or perhaps they may have taken a field trip somewhere for a few weeks. Exceptions to this are those zoologists like George Schaller, Jane Goodall, or the late Diane Fossey, who literally lived side-by-side for a substantial period of time with a given species of animal, and consequently acquired first-hand knowledge of them. Only in the late sixties had this new breed of zoologist begun to emerge.

At six months of age Molly still had the "teddy bear" look.

What's going on in there?

CHAPTER 9

SNOW BEAR

Our first snowfall came in December and to Molly it was more of a nuisance than anything else. The sun bear comes from a tropical climate and does not hibernate like most other bears. The cold weather did not bother her, for Molly's coat was heavy enough, but there was nothing for her to do. She climbed the barren trees but usually came back down after a few minutes.

It was heartbreaking to see her turning over rocks in a futile quest of insects which were no longer to be found in the frozen ground. She would go from one rock to the next, seemingly unable to understand why there were no ants and beetles where there once had been. I couldn't wait for spring to come with its renaissance of life which would restore what Molly was longing for.

Without much to hold her interest outside, Molly usually came back to her room fairly soon, and I was obliged to spend a good deal more time playing with her inside. We had several games which she liked immensely; in one, she would curl up in an automobile tire (which was left in her room) after which I would come over and maul with her. After wrestling around together I would break away and walk to the corner of the room. Moll would immediately return to the tire, knowing that was a signal to bring me back for more play. Over and over we would repeat the cycle.

The amazing thing about the tire game was that Molly learned it in five minutes. I had only to go through the routine three or four times, and she caught on right away. She could play it endlessly, never seeming to tire of the repetition. She was simple indefatigable; I was not, so when I was completely worn out after half an hour or more of frolic, I would put some cookies on her shelf and make a tactful exit while she was heading for them. Even this exit format became a regular routine—all part of the game.

Once in a while I would bring Bogo down to Moll's room to let them play, but unfortunately the enjoyment was unilateral. Molly, of course, thoroughly delighted in the roughhousing, but Bogo never appreciated it. Inevitably he found himself hemmed into a corner before the tank-lime advance of Molly, and he would then explode on her in a defensive rage of near bites from which she would tuck her head under her paws—and still keep coming. I noticed that she was always sure to cover her little ears, a habit probably acquired when she played the same game with Betsy who always gave Moll's ears a vigorous nipping.

When Molly would roll into a shell from the dog's attack, she always reminded me of Lenny the feebleminded giant in "Of Mice and Men," who would cover up and plead for help even though he was much bigger and stronger than his tormentors. In fairness to Bogo I had to cut the encounter short since it was nothing but aggravation for him. He was outweighed some eighty pounds and had much less stamina than the bear, besides deriving no pleasure from it anyway. Molly just loved the game, so with Bogo usually unavailable, the only other maulable foil was I. After each nightly mauling session, I definitely had no problems falling asleep.

Another indoor diversion of Molly's was playing on the cellar stairs and banister. Here the frolic consisted of climbing in and out of the banister and stretching out to bite my hands as I reached for her. Of course, to come around the side of the stairs and stand beneath Molly was a sure invitation to get dropped on and mauled. In such cases I had to exercise care not to get bitten on the head because Molly seemed to regard hair as sort of fur, which seemed a natural place to bite. She didn't realize that the hair was no protection at all, and many times I felt the long canine teeth against my head—a very painful experience.

In cold weather the customary finger-biting frolicking also posed a problem; in fact, it was downright punishment, because even a playful bite on cold fingers would really hurt. Nevertheless, I tried to endure it as best I could rather than eliminate a well-established pattern of communication.

Actually, if Molly were to accidentally hurt an arm or finger, she always knew it from the victim's flinching and would let up immediately. Or if I were to yell "Ow!" she stopped at once and became visibly repentant, stepping away and then slowly backing into me, first making contact with her rump and then gradually bringing the side and head around. I believe this backward approach was an instinctive gesture to show friendliness—the idea being that the jaws were held out of the way. Such logic is characteristic in the animal world; a similar trait can be seen in various antelopes that will signify a friendly approach to a contemporary by deliberately holding the head high so the horns are back and obviously less threatening.

Devoting so much time to our little bear was all an integral part of the commitment imposed on me once I had made the decision to keep a wild animal. If Molly were ever to relate to humans it could only come about by her being with them as much as possible.

The degree to which this concept worked can be appreciated by the fact that Molly actually responded to petting, a supreme—and rare—phenomenon for a wild animal. She would lie placidly in her automobile tire on her back, and allow me to stroke from the side of her neck straight down over her chest, while she eyed me intently with paws dangling in a marionette-like pose. The usual reaction would have been for her to swat my hands away, along with biting gestures, but she actually came to welcome my stroking her chest. I was very proud of this achievement and considered it to be one of the most significant milestones in my efforts to bridge the communication gap.

A yearly ritual with our family each winter was the building of snow animals. After a good snowfall (which has become a rarity these last few years) the Samuels' lawn would soon be adorned with elephants, bears, dogs and other animals stoically awaiting the neighborhood children to visit, sit on them and play their games of make-believe. In honor of Molly, my first figure that year was a bear. It was about six feet tall and showed the bear in the two-legged upright stance which any bear is capable of assuming. After it was completed, I poured chocolate water on it to give it a realistic brown color (it was not a sun bear).

Molly's reaction was captivating. She came over to it very deliberately, rose on her hind legs like the subject in question, and gave it a thorough sniffing. It was not the fact that the chocolate water carried a specific scent; Molly was just investigating in the general way she always did with any new object or animal. She then just put her paws on the sides of the snow bear's arms and began to climb it.

I managed to record all this in 8mm color movies; the most splendid scene came at one point when Molly lingered for a few moments nose to nose with her contemporary of snow. After the examination was over, Molly dropped down and moved on.

Even though the statue was frozen hard Molly's claws did do some damage but I was pleased to see that it did support her weight, all 105 pounds of her.

When we show the film, I always stop it at the point where their noses are touching; what a dramatic scene it makes. I have tried many times to have a still picture made from the film clip, but no one seems to be able to do it. It is the picture that I was hoping to use for the cover of this book. Oh well, someday photographic technology will be advanced enough for me to get this picture—it's worth waiting for.

SNOW BEAR

SNOW ANIMALS

SNOW BEAR

SNOW BEAR

CHAPTER 10

PLUMBER NEEDED

One day I got the bright idea of putting linoleum on the floor in Molly's room. Knowing that she would try to rip it up I nailed a border of wooden planks around the room so the edges could not be reached.

I was quite pleased with the way the linoleum enhanced the appearance of the room. Furthermore, it would provide a more comfortable floor for me when Molly and I played our mauling games. Ha! What a pipedream! In fifteen minutes, the linoleum was ripped to shreds—an hour and a half's work of cutting, fitting and hammering was all for naught. She simply clawed away methodically at one point until a breach was made; after that it was an easy matter to rip up the rest of the material.

Iris gave me one of the "I told you so" looks, and she was right. I should have realized that the "engine of destruction" named "Molly" would promptly do what she did best, "search and destroy."

A bear is like a crowbar with a brain. Nothing is safe from them. Their ingenuity at reaching out-of-the way places is astonishing. Objects which you would swear they could not reach are broken when you return, and often you have no idea how it could have happened. For example, the light fixture in the middle of the ceiling seemed safe enough from her curiosity, but Molly took care of that the first time her bureau was in the vicinity. Luckily there were no electrical repercussions from the destruction.

I once had occasion to board up a high portion of a wall Molly had damaged. I remember thinking at the time that the repair should be sturdy enough to endure for at least a few months. How wrong I was. Half an hour later we re-entered her room and found it once again wrecked. I am still not sure how she negotiated that one, but I do know that upon seeing me she had her usual innocent manner. The kissed and chirping came forth as if she were trying to say, "You love me no matter what I do or how much work I cause you." And it was true—I just couldn't get angry at her.

Moll was often attracted to her window, and many times it was necessary for me to board up the access to the window (not the window itself) or else she would have gone right through, glass and all.

It was clear that these ramblings did not represent any intention to escape from her room because she may have disliked it; in fact there were three occasions when Molly pushed open her window and went outside and, instead of running into the woods as she would do when I took her out, she stayed by the window and was preoccupied with the problem of how to get back in.

Even zoo animals are often hesitant to leave their usual quarters if suddenly given an open door. Their familiar haven represents a welcome security from which they are reluctant to part. I should say here that nothing is more repugnant to me than the thought of a caged animal. If there must be zoos, at least let them be in the enlightened modern style where the bars and cages are replaced by a more natural setting. Some old time zoo keepers claim that the animals are just as content in the box cages as an open moated area, that it is the spectators who appreciate the sense of freedom more, but I disagree. One way to assess animals' relative contentment in captivity is in their propensity to breed. Open type zoos are achieving much better results than the old-style zoos in this area, particularly with some endangered species like the snow leopard. I recall one night when Molly worked her way out of her room and must have lingered outside for at least ten minutes before I was aware of it. Not knowing what to do next she had moved up to the porch and was about to enter the house through the rear door. When I confronted her, she was so happy to see me that she kissed me profusely while providing the "chirping" serenade which always accompanied this affection.

There was one catastrophe that Moll caused in her room when she managed to rip the radiator away from the wall thereby breaking the pipes. It happened during the winter when the radiator was in service, and created a spectacular mess.

Hot water poured out flooding the floor, while billows of steam felled the room, transforming it into a veritable Turkish bath. Molly had fled to the safety of the upper shelf where she peered out with a quizzical expression reflecting complete innocence.

As luck would have it, all this took place on a Saturday night which, of course, made the problem of repairs an even more formidable challenge. The first thing to do was to turn off the heating circulator. This also shut off the heat for the house, but at least it stopped the water from pouring into the room.

Next came the problem of finding a plumber. I tried the Yellow Pages but with no success; there was simply no help to be had at that hour on such short notice. The best I could do was to get someone to come the next morning (Sunday). Meanwhile it looked as if we were in for a rugged night— the temperature was around 20°. Normally we could have held out for the night with extra clothes and blankets; however, one of the children had a cold—unfortunate timing indeed.

The situation was finally resolved when the oil burner man, after first claiming that the problem was way out of his realm, agreed to come over on his way home and try to install a temporary fix which would hold us until the plumber arrived.

I had the problem of keeping Molly occupied in the main cellar for an hour while the man worked in her room. When he first noticed her, he was quite frightened, but soon saw she was not a threat. She refused to stay in the cellar for any long intervals, however, and kept getting in the way, being her usual nosy self. She certainly would not allow a nice big tool box to go without a thorough checkout. As a matter of fact, Howard was the same way—in terms of curiosity, bears and two-year-old boys have a lot in common.

The repairman finally succeeded in stalling valves on the ends of the two broken pipes. They were the type with adjusting levers where the rate of flow could be varied by hand—or paw—as it turned out. Naturally as soon as we left the room Molly assumed the role of field inspector which involved climbing over the fallen radiator and turning the levers on again! I had to tie the levers with wire to prevent their being reopened. This arrangement managed to hold for the night, but the next morning I could see that the wires were considerably deformed from the pressure of Molly's further efforts.

The plumber was a welcome sight as he arrived on what must have been his most unusual call. Again, I had to keep Molly occupied for an hour or so, though she periodically returned to the room to check whether she was missing anything interesting. More than once I had to lift her front paws off the plumber's back where her curiosity had brought her for the usual inspection. She also had to be exiled during the welding operations, when she definitely would have been in the way.

Finally, all the repairs were made; this time the radiator was bolted to the wall by heavy clamping bands. The heating system was back to normal; and Molly, of course, acted as if nothing had happened, and there was a plumber who had serendipitously acquired the best story of his career.

At home in the woods.

CHAPTER 11

A FRIEND IN THE WOODS

With the coming of spring Molly's weight had reached 120 pounds, at which point it began to level off. Her coat was a beautiful glossy black, its texture hardy from the winter months.

The lure of the woods was returning and the fat little bear began to stray in them for increasingly longer periods. About half the time was spent up in the trees nibbling at leaf buds or just clawing bark, while the other half found her on the ground foraging for insects which were starting to reappear. An overturned rock would suddenly expose a black beetle. In a flash the long tongue would zip out and the insect was consumed. Small red ants along with clusters of larvae were to be found, and this delicacy also suited Molly's diet as long as the supply held out. Thus, the two acres of woods were an ideal setting for Molly. It was similar to the terrain she would have in her native Malaysia. In the Malay language the sun bear is described as *bagindo nan tinggih*—the literal translation is "his majesty who is high up," which refers to their sitting in the trees much of the time.

SEARCHING FOR INSECTS
Among the rocks.

A FRIEND IN THE WOODS

In rotting tree trunks.

A FRIEND IN THE WOODS

Emerging from the woods after a lengthy session there.

"Chirp, chirp, chirp, chirp..."

Molly being her usual cooperative self.

OTHER ANIMAL FRIENDS Anoa
(See page 60)

Baby dingo (Australian wild dog)

Iris with anoa and same dingo

Lion cub

Rhino (See page 17)

Baby giraffe.

Bears that are semi-dependent of humans, as Molly was, are always happiest in familiar surroundings. They get used to seeing the same people, same yard, same objects, using the same trails, etc., and from such repetition there is less to be frightened of.

The only time Molly would stray from her usual grounds was when a dog (usually Bogo) would come by and lure her away. Even if she were thirty feet up in a tree, when Bogo appeared, she would hurriedly descend in order to scamper after him. This caused a problem at times because the dog would often lead her far away and then lose her. I would have to trail behind to keep track of her whereabouts. It wasn't easy to stay near when Molly was in a hurry, for she could thread her way through the dense foliage must faster than I could.

It was never clear to me why Moll preferred to follow Bogo rather than Betsy. Betsy had always been a much better companion, but it was the male dog who intrigued her. Maybe it was his aloof manner, for he never was much interested in her attention. It wasn't because she was a bear, in fact he behaved exactly the same way with own offspring. He just wasn't that sociable.

Bordering the edge of our land was an estate occupied by the Schultz family, who had a large German Shepherd dog. It was a handsome four-year-old male with the somewhat intimidating name of Storm; actually, the name was a misnomer, for the dog had a friendly temperament, not having been conditioned to be otherwise. Many German Shepherd owners seem to believe that the dog's destiny is merely to serve as a watchdog automaton, but happily that was not the case here.

We saw Storm only occasionally, perhaps three or four times a year when he would come through the back woods briefly to visit our dogs. Mr. Schultz had met Molly during

some of our jaunts in the woods, and like
the other neighbors he found her interesting
and friendly. He was, however, a little
dubious about what would happen if the dog
and bear should ever meet. It was his
opinion that a fight would erupt, but I
disagreed. After all, it takes two to tangle
and Molly had absolutely no such
inclination. Furthermore, if anything scared
her, she would simply head for the nearest
tree, and watch the proceedings safely
perched high above her grounded adversary.

MOLLY AT ONE YEAR
Automobile inspection

Rendezvous for cookies at the top of the ladder. (See page 25)

The daily climb.

Typical view from the bedroom window.

Molly shown with Betsy (left) and Bogo. The characteristic "V" chest mark can be seen. She didn't really ride the bicycle.

A FRIEND IN THE WOODS

It was inevitable that Molly and Storm would encounter each other someday, and it finally came to pass one summer afternoon. The dog had made one of his infrequent excursions through the woods near our grounds, and Molly had just come down from a half hour stay in a tree. The timing was perfect.

They were about twenty feet apart when they spied each other, and the staring contest promptly began. I watched from well off to the side with no intention of interfering, for I knew it was best for them to meet by themselves. Most accidental confrontations which occur in the animal world rarely have serious consequences to either party. Usually they end up with each going his own way, or if one concedes the superiority of the other, that is enough to end matters.

While I was contemplating this scenario, I couldn't help thinking how far removed it seemed from the surrounding residential world. How oblivious the shoppers in the Armonk A&P were to the unlikely meeting taking place in the woods less than two miles away from them.

There they were, sizing each other up, ursine and canine—the bear from the jungles of southeastern Asia and the dog whose ancestors had established a rapport with man thousands of years ago. The dog stood still with a puzzled look while Molly took a few steps towards him, then froze again. Molly was certainly used to dogs, having been brought up with them, but the sudden appearance of one in the woods had a dramatic effect on her. She acted utterly spellbound. Her small eyes gazed intently while the chunky body was crouched, motionless, ready to plunge ahead. As the dog continued to stare, Molly finally decided to have a first-hand look, and charged right up to him.

They sniffed each other nose-to-nose for about eight seconds, and apparently each passed the all-important smell test. Just then Betsy ran up to Storm with her stubby tail wagging—big flirt that she always was. This was no means their first meeting, as evidenced by the half-shepherd, half-terrier pups she had produced after a "mishap" two years before.

Storm briefly acknowledged her greeting, and then became totally indifferent to the proceedings. As far as he was concerned there was nothing that warranted any more of his valuable time, so he just turned around and ambled back through the woods towards his house.

Molly, however, had other ideas. The big dog thoroughly fascinated her, so predictably she bounded after him followed by Betsy, while I brought up the rear, yelling, "Stop!Come back!" which I knew was a ludicrous exhibition in futility. This four-unit procession must have been a bizarre sight to any eyes in the woods that might have been watching. It was dog, bear, dog, man, in that order—the Armonk Handicap. And a handicap it was, for beside having two less legs than the other participants, I was certain that any minute I would stumble into a yellowjackets' nest and thereby add those unwelcome contestants to the race.

Before long the dogs and bear were out of sight and only the rustling noises in the bushes signaled their presence far ahead. Most of those sounds were due to Molly, who was more prone to crashing through dense brush than were the dogs. A bear is built like a tank and sometimes acts accordingly, with its straight-ahead-at-all-costs philosophy, particularly when on a mission such as this one.

By now the animals had reached a clearing and all was quiet. As I labored through the last 100 feet of woods, I wondered what I would find. A short rock wall ran along the border of the woods adjacent to the back grounds of the Schultz's house. Climbing this, I looked into the yard and, lo and behold, saw—nothing! No dogs, bears or people were in sight. The house seemed empty and there was no car in the driveway so at least I didn't have to explain Molly's impromptu visit to anyone.

As for finding her, that was not too difficult. Knowing her ways, the first place to look would be up in the trees. Of course, even if you had the right tree you couldn't always spot her immediately, because sometimes she would disappear into the heavy summer foliage. I had, however, become quite experienced in locating her under these conditions by noting familiar sounds and movements in the tree. On occasion I would amuse guests by pointing to a spot in the trees where the bear was, while they couldn't understand how I knew.

In this case the first tree I checked turned out to be the right one. It was a large oak situated midway between the rock wall and the house, and there sitting thirty feet up was Molly.

She was predictably engrossed in nibbling the bark and paid no attention to me calling her. This posed no immediate problem however, as there was a reliable way to get her down in such situations. The trick was to call Betsy over and then have the two of us leave, but it had to be done convincingly. If I moved away from the tree hesitatingly, she would know what I was doing and would not come down, or after she was down if I looked back as if to welcome her, the mischievous girl would immediately flee in another direction. The idea was to make her think she was chasing us and on this occasion our acting must have been believable, for Molly descended the tree and bounded after us.

If I allowed her to overtake me (sometimes involuntarily in the heavier brush) she would often bite my leg in passing. The bite was also accompanied by some mauling swipes with her paws, all done in a hit-and-run fashion so as to avid my retaliatory swipe which she knew would be forthcoming. It was often difficult to convince others that such actions on the part of the bear were *friendly* overtures, but they were. Biting gestures are one of the bear's main methods of communication; the way in which it is done is all-important. Check this the next time you go to a zoo (if you must).

After Molly, Betsy and I returned home I told Iris and the girls of Molly's meeting with Storm. They thought it was a beautiful adventure. If I had only had my camera with me when they were face to face—what a picture it would have made! Many times after that I did take the camera when we roamed the woods, hoping for a repeat encounter, but was never lucky enough to catch such a perfect scene. There was only one other time that I know of when Molly and Storm met again. It was during the following spring at which time Molly had demonstrated her seasonal awareness by digging for dormant caterpillar-like things which were buried in the dark earth near the base of some large trees.

While she was busy excavating, the dog came by and saw Molly who stopped for a few seconds to look at him, then promptly resumed the digging. The delicacy of these insects was too great to allow her to be sidetracked. Anyway, it was apparent that the two animals were well acquainted by now, and I suspected that they probably had met at other times I was unaware of. This was quite possible, inasmuch as I didn't keep

Molly within sight at all times; it wasn't as necessary as it had been in the early months, since she always returned when she was ready.

How nice it would have been if the dog had accepted the bear as a playmate to be visited regularly, but such storybook endings are associated with human desires and not so relevant in the animal world. Nevertheless, Molly always loved to roam the woods, and seemed to be delightfully fulfilled each time she would return from them, make her way into her room and curl up on her favorite shelf for some cookies followed by a well-earned nap.

Daily mauling play. Molly is full-grown here, weighing 125 pounds.

CHAPTER 12

BEAR LOGIC

Bears are easy to bribe. They'll do anything for a handout, and they catch on right away regarding what is necessary to keep the food coming. This is why they can be found in circuses riding bicycles, ice skating, balancing on a rolling ball, working seesaws, or engaged in various other manipulations normally performed by humans. Few in the audience notice the instant reward surreptitiously being slipped in the ursine's mouth following each local routine. In almost every case the payola is given on the spot and cannot be postponed until the animals are back in their quarters.

A quality that one cannot help noticing in a bear is its overwhelmingly honest, innocent personality. There is nothing subtle or sneaky about bears. They are completely straightforward in their intentions. If their objective, for example, is to get from point A to point B, they only know one path—the shortest distance between them. Unlike cats, for instance, bears use the direct approach; anything that happens to be in their way gets either pushed over, climbed, dismantled or, not infrequently, a combination of all three. Barriers, whether they are objects or people, mean nothing. If Molly saw a ladder it was invariably climbed; any person who happened to be on the ladder was either shoved aside or climbed over.

As Molly was growing, I tried to adapt her to living with us in a semi-domestic state. It was my hope that she would be capable of staying in the main rooms of the house like a dog or cat that sits by one's side. This turned out to be an impossibility; Moll could not be taught to remain in a passive state. Left alone she would devastate a room in a manner of minutes. Lamps would be knocked over, upholstery torn, drawers pulled out and emptied, furniture climbed on... The proverbial bull in a china shop had nothing on our Molly-Pie.

The one place where Molly would lie relaxed was on the shelf in her room. After a hard play session, she would return to the shelf, eat some cookies, then rest her chin on her forepaws and chirp softly; she hadn't a care in the world. In no time at all, she would be asleep in a curled-up position, her head tucked well under her paws as though covering up her ears against noise.

It was interesting to note that while Molly, in general, was completely oblivious to whether something would break, spill, or tip over, when she was in a tree she knew enough to avoid sitting on rotten branches, which would not have held her weight. Some kind of instinctive awareness was apparently present.

For some reason Molly was afraid of the sound of sawing wood. Whenever she heard it (on those occasions when I had to do some reinforcing in her room) she would flee to her upper shelf, which to her represented the greatest security.

Curiously enough, the hammering of nails, which was much louder than sawing, never bothered her. In fact, she took it as an invitation to stick her nose right in the way, greatly hampering the work being done.

It was a special treat for Molly when Bonnie had her birthday party the first winter the cub was with us. After the party was collected all the unfinished ice cream and cake and deposited in in front of Moll, and how she loved it! As she happily gorged herself the children, mostly five-year-olds, all crowded around and petted her. Under normal circumstances she would not relate to such petting and would shy away from it, but with the delicious treat she was too preoccupied with feasting to be concerned with anything else.

Bears traditionally love honey but I rarely gave Molly any beacuse it always made her too loose. Wirth the large number of cookies she was ingesting, it just made her sugar content that much higher.

My technique for weighing Molly when she was full grown was similar to the method often used to weigh dogs, where the person stands on the scale holding the dog then subtracts his own weight.

In the beginning I used to hold Molly under the chest and forepaws, but after she reached one hundred pounds, I had to take some weight off my arms by holding her thick neck fur in my teeth. That technique never hurt her; in fact, it made things easier, for she would cooperate—a rarity for her—by hanging perfectly limp without wiggling thereby allowing me to get the reading fairly easily. My facility at lifting her was reminiscent of the legend about the farm boy who lifted his calf every day until it became a full-grown cow. Although Molly's weight was not that great, others who were invited to try (even weight-lifter types) had great difficulty budging her. I

think their problem was partly physical—
not knowing where the center of gravity
was—and party psychological—knowing
where the teeth were.

By the time she reached adulthood
Molly had fully adjusted to her semi-
artificial life with us. She was healthy and
happy, eating well, climbing, and foraging—
the very things a sun bear should be doing.
Companionship was the vital ingredient for
the ability to live with people, even though,
in the wild, long term companionship is
foreign to bears; they are solitary animals
during most of their adult lives. It is only
for a two to three week spell out of the
entire year that the male stays with the
female, then they go their separate ways.
The next spring if they should happen to
meet, he will find her quite changed. No
longer sexually captivating as before, and
accompanied by his own offspring in the
form of small cubs, she will be governed by
her protective instinct, and this same lady
with whom he spent that honeymoon the
previous summer will growl a "...stay
away!" warning that foreshadows an
explosion of teeth and claws if he should
venture too near. More likely, however, any
such encounter will be avoided for the
mother bear, upon detecting the scent

(or other signs) of the male will scrupulously lead her family away to avoid any confrontation.

In another year, however, he will be back in the fickle sow's good graces again, and it will then be the one-and-a-half-year-old cubs, now weighing over a hundred pounds, who are driven away as their mother once more seeks a mate. The larger bears such as the brown bear or polar bear generally wait at least two years before mating again.

Bears can live together in groups when they have to, as happens in zoos, where breeding is not uncommon for some types of bear. The sun bear is an exception, however, practically never giving birth in captivity, though I think this could probably be remedied by providing a more favorable environment. The miserable box cage used by most zoos certainly cannot be conducive to breeding. Since tree climbing is such an all-important part of the sun bear's daily routine it should be made available in the form of a small patch of woods. Some zoos do provide artificial tree sections but they are not a satisfactory substitute. The real thing, complete with foliage, is needed and, in my opinion, would make a big difference in breeding results.

BEAR LOGIC

Larger bears do tend to maul trees in zoos, which eventually destroys the trees, but this would not happen so readily with the sun bear. In this country the Cleveland Zoo as well as the renowned San Diego Zoo are among the very few that have recorded births of sun bears. The most success worldwide, up to now, comes from the Berlin-Friedrichfelde Zoo which has succeeded in rearing several litters since the early nineteen sixties.

Philosophically speaking, it may be just as well that few sun bears are born in zoos; after all a zoo is nothing more than a jail for animals. Some are worse than others but they all, without exception, deprive the animal of the most precious commodity in the world—freedom. The relatively open-type zoos at least make an attempt to restore some space to their captives even though their mode of existence is still artificial. The old way of keeping animals in a small cage, unfortunately still prevalent throughout the world, must be classified as obscene, nothing short of a blot upon our alleged "civilization."

It is a grim and ironic testimony to man's destructiveness, intentional or otherwise, that some species no longer exist in the world and have escaped extinction only by breeding in zoos.

Man has dominated, unforgivably abused, and unconsciously exterminated many of the wild animals which shared this planet with him. He has forced the interrelationship to exist as a competition in which his superior intellect has become a ruthless weapon. One need only consider the long list of mammals, birds and fish which have disappeared, never again to be seen. They have fallen from the life cycle, victims of extinction, that irreversible process in which there is no second chance.

Certainly increasing lack of space caused by the inexorable human population explosion, as well as its ever-present by-product, pollution, is the greatest indirect threat to wildlife, but besides these involuntary processes, outright, willful cruelty is still rampant throughout the world. A grim example is that degenerate orgy of sadism known as "bullfighting"—a spectacle of Middle Ages barbarism (where plunging steel into living flesh and blood constitutes a perverse entertainment) still lingers on in some places.

Much of the rhetoric pertaining to wildlife has been oriented to show the animal strictly as an adversary—the idea being to generate rip-roaring adventure which has always made marketable reading material chiefly due to man's ego-building needs. We have been taught to slay dragons, but in order to slay a dragon one must first create a dragon. Thus, the Hemingways, Ruarks, and Theodore Roosevelt (of the panda-shooting Roosevelts) attempted to glorify the destruction of wildlife as something admirable and heroic. From such motives the term "sportsman" has evolved. This label is one of the master euphemisms of all time. It identifies in noble terms that inferior feeling individual, oblivious to cruelty, who finds it fulfilling to shoot bullets (or other things)—at defenseless animals, from a safe distance, with a high powered weapon, usually with armed companions standing by—didn't you know—they call it "harvesting." In reality the "sportsman" myth is perpetuated by the many business which thrive on its image and cater to the hoary mentalities which sustain it.

They insist they are merely helping to "maintain the balance" but this fraudulent claim is readily exposed by the existence of the many "hunting preserves" where the "sportsman" pay admission to hunt in a fenced area, stocked with animals just for that purpose. It's great when they never shoot back. Hunters despise "Bambi." They consider the story representative of a syndrome which fosters naïve sentimentality towards animals, but they have never objected to "Little Red Riding Hood" which promulgates the myth that wolves eat people.

How ironic it is that the Adamsons of "Born Free" fame, Joy and George, who spent much of their adult lives in the company of "man-eating lions" were eventually killed, not by these lions, but by fellow humans. The same is true of Diane Fossey, who lived among supposedly ferocious gorillas (an egregious myth perpetuated by the King Kong syndrome) only to fall prey to another human being.

Perhaps if more people understood the innocent, self-contained world of bears there would be less desire to shoot them for so-called "sport." Admittedly, it would not make much difference to some "sportsmen" since the lust to kill wildlife for entertainment (the "sportsman" never can distinguish this from eating meat) is a strong atavistic trait in many individuals. Anyone who harbors an intimate awareness and feeling for animals can only regard the "sport" of hunting as a senseless, repugnant indulgence in refined sadism. Even to call this contemptible carnage "brutal" or "savage" is to slander the "brutes" (wild animals) and primitive peoples, neither of whom hunt except to feed or clothe themselves, i.e., out of necessity. Killing for the sheer pleasure is almost entirely a disease in civilized man, like alcoholism or schizophrenia—but that subject deserves a whole book to itself. Two convincing studies of this malady are, *"Death as a Way of Life" by Roger Caras (Little, Waltham, Mass., 1971), "Man Kind?" by Cleveland Amory (Harper Row, New York, 1974).*

It never fails that when a wild animal causes an accident there is a combination of fascination and outrage. Retaliation is so easy against the unequal animal, not unlike the parent who punitively overreacts against the small child during a moment of lost temper.

The accidents in Glacier National Park in the mid-sixties where two people had fatal encounters with grizzly bears received the most sensational notoriety possible. Newspapers and magazines screamed out the fearsome details in front page headlines-as if the grizzly's public image weren't already bad enough.

Certainly, the tragedy has to be deplored, and to this day no one knows for sure what caused the campers to be attacked, but its impact should be kept in perspective. Those were the only fatalities caused by grizzles in over fifty years in the park. One must conclude that it was not really the loss of life that was the major concern, so much as how it came about.

Even the grizzly's Latin name, *ursus horribilis*, is blatantly suggestive, biased, incriminating. Were it up to me I would have synthesized a more deserving name for this wonder of nature, such as *ursus "magnificus."*

As this is being edited six* people per day are dying in New York City from man-made violence, mostly drug related. On June 20, 1989, the New York City police department reported *eighteen* people killed from crime-related causes. Each year throughout the country 65,000 people will die from auto accidents—one every nine minutes—not to mention millions injured— and yet these monstrous statistics are numbly accepted as part of the life pattern. At one point in the seventies everyone was worrying about sharks! Society will take stringent measures to prevent the freak accident, but will be casually resigned to the predictable, recurring, common place disasters which account for so many more lives.

(1995)—When this book was started in the seventies, the figure was three.

CHAPTER 13

END OF A DREAM

Another spring had come. It was now two years since Molly had joined us as a little five-pound cub, at which time she so resembled a child's toy. The relationship slowly changed from priorities of mutual accommodation to an established routine. At times I wondered if the never-ending commitment to provide daily side-by-side companionship might drift into a hardship.

Occasionally it was a strain, even for me; I would just plain run out of energy. There could never be a day off. Vacations or even an overnight absence were impossible since the morning feeding and the romp in the woods were always expected. One time I was in the midst of a bout with stomach virus and barely able to make it down the stairs, yet I had to drag myself to Molly's room for our daily mauling. The thought of her waiting in vain was too much to bear (no pun).

One evening I was unexpectedly an hour late returning home from work, to discover that Molly had literally gone through the wall searching for me. In her efforts to find out why I wasn't on schedule she had pried open some wooden wall panels and gone right through the plaster boards. Had she been outside at the time it would not have mattered for she simply would have reversed the process, tearing at the walls to get in.

Such was the ironclad responsibility that had evolved or, more exactly, that I had taken on and because of it, uncertainties of the future now began to plague me. I tried desperately to shut out those negative thoughts which might lead to the terrifying conclusion that it would not be fair to keep Molly with us indefinitely. But it became more and more difficult. In the end I finally had to face the cold, hard reality of the situation; one of these was my own conscience, which reminded me that I must do what was best for our bear, regardless if my own feelings. It was the end of the world for me, but Molly's long-term welfare had to come first.

What was the answer? To me a zoo is a synonym for a prison for animals. Even the more modern ones without cages are a poor substitute for life in the wild as nature intended it to be. I must confess I have grown to avoid them, since I can no longer stand to see an animal in a cage.

END OF A DREAM

For Molly, I finally found a solution, the only decent one I could think of: an animal farm down south; it seemed to be the best thing available. I suppose it wasn't that different from a zoo except for more freedom of space, less exposure to the public. At least there wouldn't be long insectless winters where countless rocks would be turned over in a vain search for ants or beetles which were nowhere to be found.

It was the time in the late 1960's when the Beatles' hit song "Hey Jude" was at the height of its popularity. We heard it daily, and as songs sometimes become associated with some person, event or situation, so I deeply identified "Hey Jude" with Molly's presence.

Each time I heard it, it would remind me of some characteristic Molly-type situation: bounding across the backyard headed for the woods, or where the rays of the rising sun produced an exquisite golden orange on her chest marking. Most of all, though, the song brought me back to the evenings in her room where the hours of mauling, resting, and side-by-side togetherness forged a lasting bond between us.

"Hey Jude, don't make it bad—take a sad song and make it bet-ter..." But nothing in my life was ever sadder or more devastating than the thought of Molly's leaving, even though I knew it was for her own good. The beautiful dream was only temporary after all. "...Remember to let her into your heart..." That was what I had done, and that was where she had gone—on a one-way trip. April 21, 1969, was the worst day of my life; part of me died that day. My mind was in a daze for weeks after. Illusions of Molly tormented me when I looked up into the trees in the twilight hours. I couldn't believe she was really gone.

The signs were around for years—the scars, bare of bark, visible at discrete points in various trees, the shingles missing by the kitchen window, the mangled remains of our hapless cherry tree, her favorite shelf—now empty—where she would rest her face on her paws and emit that soft whimpering of contentment. It still hurts to think of her. What I'd give for one more bite from those self-righteous jaws! Let it even be in the winter on frozen fingers—it still wouldn't hurt as much as the memory of her. This book took ten years to write because of the painful recollection of wonderful times and then eventual parting which was such a terrible ordeal.

Please don't anyone else do it. This applies to all wild animals, especially those which are imported such as ocelots, margays, monkeys, kinkajous (honey bears), exotic birds and reptiles. Each year hundreds of thousands of these animals die supplying a system where the few that do survive will be bought by some show-off who will end up disposing of the animal once the novelty has worn off, usually within less than a year. Each purchase of an exotic animal just serves to perpetuate the abuses of the "pet" industry.

Arm in arm—our last picture together.

Article From The New York Times, 1994

"Southeast Asia, with its abundant rainfall and high temperatures, is home to a great diversity of sun-loving animal and plant species. To help promote the protection of the many endangered animals, Singapore has issued a special "animal series" dedicated to Southeast Asia mammals.

The first in the set is a 20-cent stamp featuring the Sun Bear. They are the smallest members of the bear family. Sun Bears are primarily forest dwellers and nocturnal in habit. The cute little ones become dangerous when full grown."

EPILOGUE

Life goes on.

I no longer keep in touch with the animal farm. I did, for the first two years after Molly's departure, to assure myself that she was in good hands; then it was better not to be reminded. For a while I used to get the doleful questions, "Say, how's your bear?" to which I would offer the laconic response, "She's fine," and discreetly change the subject as quickly as possible. But fortunately, they don't ask so often these days. In the beginning I had to endure the thoughtlessly crude inquiries of those who had heard that I "got rid of" my bear. It was then explained that I NEVER "got rid of" her, as if I were forced to because she had become unmanageable or such. No neighborhood petitions were circulated, the police were never called, nor was there any other reason except for my own agonized decision to do what was best for her in the long run.

EPILOGUE

It couldn't be done again. Aside from the unfairness-to-the-animal factor, in one's lifetime it is difficult to summon the energy to repeat a long-term project requiring such intense dedication. The physical and emotional drain would just be overwhelming. It took years for the "scars" from the first episode to heal (though never fully).

As for the children—the memory has faded. Howard remembers nothing since he was not yet three when she left. Bonnie, more than anything else, remembers the play sessions every evening in Molly's room before bedtime (Molly's). She also recalls, as a four-year-old, being pushed into the small backyard pool by a lurching Molly during some picture taking efforts. The memory is particularly vivid because she wearing her new dress. Adrienne of course remembers more, such as the ant collections in the margarine bowl for a Molly meal, and being greeted by Molly after getting off the school bus.

Someday they'll tell their children they had a real bear for a pet whom they adored. As adults they, like other genuine animal lovers, realize that the ultimate act of kindness to a wild animal is to leave it alone in its natural habitat—free.

Our family—1973.

Our family—1982.

Our family—2019

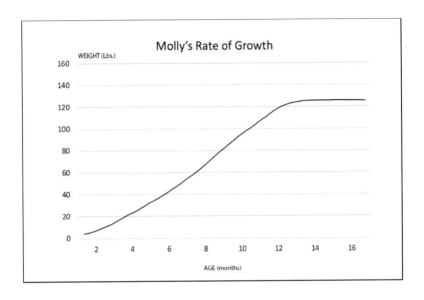

Molly's Rate of Growth

WEIGHT (Lbs.)

AGE (months)

DANIEL SAMUELS

Daniel Samuels grew up in Mt. Vernon, N.Y. and is a graduate of the University of Pennsylvania. Professionally he was an engineer and has taught radio and television theory.

In the sixties and seventies he was the New York District Representative for the East African Wild Life Society, and at times contributed to the wildlife magazine *Africana*, published in Nairobi. He has lectured on African wildlife.

Mr. Samuels has held the rank of Master in chess and is fluent in Spanish, Russian and Swahili. At the age of 79 he won an Over-70 boxing world championship. He and his wife, Iris, reside in Westchester County, N.Y. Three children and five grandchildren comprise the present family.

Made in the USA
Middletown, DE
09 October 2020